GREEN FILES

CLIMATE IN CRISIS

GREEN FILES – CLIMATE IN CRISIS
was produced by

David West 🧍🧍 **Children's Books**
7 Princeton Court
55 Felsham Road
London SW15 1AZ

Editor: Gail Bushnell
Picture Research: Carlotta Cooper

First published in Great Britain by Heinemann
Library, Halley Court, Jordan Hill, Oxford
OX2 8EJ, part of Harcourt Education.
Heinemann is a registered trademark
of Harcourt Education Ltd.

07 06 05 04 03
10 9 8 7 6 5 4 3 2 1

ISBN 0 431 18293 0 (HB)
ISBN 0 431 18300 7 (PB)

British Library Cataloguing in Publication Data

Parker, Steve
Climate in crisis. - (Green Files)
1. Climate changes - Juvenile literature
I. Title
363.7'3874

Printed and bound in Italy

PHOTO CREDITS :
Abbreviations: t-top, m-middle, b-bottom, r-right,
l-left, c-centre.

Front cover, tl & 19l (Sipa Press); tr, 4t & 23t - Re
Features Ltd; b, 3, 14–15 & 26b - Corbis Images.
Pages 4–5, 8t, m & b, 9tl & m, 15ml, bl, mr & br,
17m, 24t, 28r, 30 - Corbis Images. 5t, 25l, 26–27
(Sabine Vielmo); 5bl (Andy Crump); 6br, 17t, 20t,
(Mark Edwards); 7t (Roland Seitre); 9b (Shehzad
Noorani); 10m (D. Escartin); 10b (Voltchev/UNEP
11t (Klaus Andrews); 12l (Horst Schafer); 15t
(Romain Garrouste); 16b (Ron Giling); 18 (Nigel
Dickinson); 20b (Julio Etchart); 20–21 (Peres/UNE
22br (Thomas Raupach); 24b (Mathieu Laboureur
28b (Jorgen Schytte); 29bm (Dylan Garcia) - Still
Pictures. 5br & 17mr (Peter MacDiarmid); 6b, 11l
19r, 21m & b (Sipa Press); 7bl & b (2002 Eumetsa
9tr (Richard Jones); 13 (Monika Duscher); 16bl (C
Williams); 22l (Solent News and Photos); 26t (Ray
Tang); 27b (Action Press); 29r (Bryn Colton); 6–7,
12r, 18–19, 25b, 29bl - Rex Features Ltd. 27t -
NASA.

All the Internet addresses (URLs) given in this boo
were valid at the time of going to press. However,
to the dynamic nature of the Internet, some addres
may have changed, or sites may have ceased to exi
since publication. While the author and publishers
regret any inconvenience this may cause readers, n
responsibility for any such changes can be accepte
by either the author or the publishers.

*An explanation of difficult words can be
found in the glossary on page 31.*

GREEN FILES

CLIMATE IN CRISIS

Steve Parker

Heinemann
LIBRARY

CONTENTS

The 'ozone hole' (blue and red) shows where the protective gas ozone is thin, high over the South Pole. It allows more of the Sun's harmful rays through.

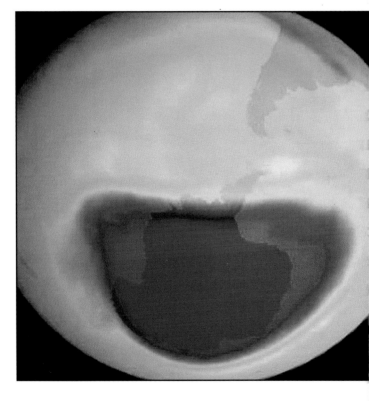

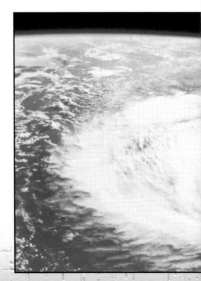

Great storms such as hurricanes are becoming more powerful, common and widespread.

INTRODUCTION

Here is the weather forecast. Tomorrow will see sleet, blizzards, snowdrifts and a wind-chill of minus 20, followed by a hurricane, heatwave and severe drought. The day after should be fine.' Our day-to-day weather is changing faster than ever. So are the general long-term patterns of weather around the world, over months and years, which are called climate. The cause is human activity, especially the smoke, fumes and chemicals we pour into the air. Can we, and our planet, cope with the crisis?

Carbon dioxide, CO_2, is one of the main greenhouse gases that cause global warming. Whenever we burn anything, we make more CO_2.

Demonstrators warn that as global warming melts polar ice, sea levels may rise enough to flood whole islands.

sea level 2005

WEATHER AND CLIMATE

Sometimes the weather changes hourly, from freezing fog to bright sunshine. At other times it stays settled for weeks. Scientists called meteorologists measure weather worldwide, to make forecasts and discover more about climate change.

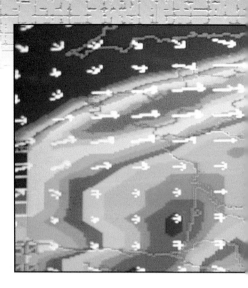

THE NEED TO KNOW

Predicting the weather is vital for many reasons – not just arranging a barbecue! Pilots, sailors, farmers, bricklayers, skiers, climbers and many others arrange their work and leisure around the weather. Ignoring it could be fatal.

Being GREEN
Even simple measurements provide valuable information for forecasting weather from places with extreme climates. The barometer detects air pressure, the hygrometer humidity, and anemometer wind speed and direction.

Harsh weather, like snowstorms in New York City, bring normal life to a halt. Disruption costs billions – and sometimes lives too.

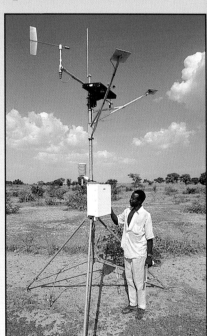

Weather station in Africa.

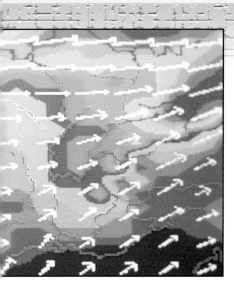

Some of the world's biggest super-computers analyze and display weather information (left).

Instruments on radiosondes ('weather balloons') radio information back to ground stations.

1 2002, a new series of weather satellites, Meteosat, were put into orbit by Ariane rockets (inset). Their cameras detect light rays, infra-red (heat), ultraviolet, radio and microwaves used for radar. These signals are then analysed in control rooms to identify weather patterns.

FROM DAYS TO CENTURIES

Meteorologists use a vast array of technologies, from simple thermometers for temperature, to billion-dollar satellites that detect rain, fog, wind patterns and the height of ocean waves to the nearest few centimetres. Day-to-day weather measurements build up to help predict longer-term changes in climate, over many years.

Climates around the world are affected by many features, from the shape of Earth and the way it goes round the Sun, to winds and ocean currents.

SHAPE OF THE PLANET

Earth is ball-shaped. The middle regions, called the tropics, are nearer the Sun and receive more warmth. The Earth also goes round the Sun not in a circle, but in an oval-like ellipse. When closest to the Sun, we have warm summers.

GLOBAL PATTERNS

As Earth spins around once each day, the Sun heats different parts by different amounts. Warm air rises, cooler air flows along to take its place, and this sets up patterns of winds. Ocean currents form in the same way.

Over thousands of years, living things have adapted to the climate in their part of the world. For example, as winds blow moist warm air over mountains, the air rises and cools. The moisture falls as rain, so lush plants can grow. As the wind blows onwards it gets drier, and the land below receives little rain, so deserts form.

Cold climates
Areas near the poles have short warm summers and long cold winters.

Dry climates
Most deserts are either side of the tropics. They receive winds which have lost all their moisture.

Polar climates
The bottom and top of the world are icy-cold all year.

Temperate climates
Midway between the poles and the Equator are warm summers and cool winters, with few extremes.

Hot topic
To survive comfortably in changing climates, all living things must adapt. Light-coloured, loose robes soak up less heat and allow air to move freely around the body, keeping it cooler.

Cool robes for the hot Sun.

Mountain climates
Temperatures fall with height. Mountains are cool in summer and freezing in winter.

Equator

TROPICS TO POLES

At midday, the Sun shines almost overhead in the tropics. Its rays are concentrated into a small area, and so they pass through less atmosphere, which means less heat loss, compared to rays at polar regions. More of the Sun's heat gets through to the surface and so tropical climates are hotter.

Polar — Sun's rays spread out.

Temperate

Sun's rays concentrated in smaller area.

Equator

Temperate

Moist tropical climates
It's warm throughout the year, and very wet in the monsoon season.

Polar — Sun's rays spread out.

9

Seasons change, mainly with warm summers and cold winters. But 200 million years ago, at the time of the dinosaurs, Earth's climate was very different. There were hardly any seasons.

CHANGES THROUGH TIME

Since Earth's beginning, 4,500 million years ago, climates have been constantly changing. Sometimes the whole world was warm and wet, and lush plants thrived in steamy swamps – even at the poles. At other times the Earth was cold all over.

Today the Sahara Desert is spreading across North Africa (main picture). Yet the cave paintings of ancient people (inset, show the Sahara region just a few thousand years ago with wild cattle and lions in woods, and even hippos and crocodiles in the rivers and swamps.

Hot topic

Some polar ice is over 4,500 metres deep, made of snow from half a million years ago. Drills bring up rod-like cores with tiny trapped air bubbles, showing the atmosphere's make-up at the time.

Sampling ice in the Arctic.

THE GREAT ICE AGE

There have been dozens of ice ages during prehistory. The last one began over 140,000 years ago. As Earth cooled, ice sheets spread from the poles across much of North America, Europe and northern Asia. Wildlife had to adapt or move south. This Great Ice Age had almost faded away 10,000 years ago.

Greatest spread of ice sheets

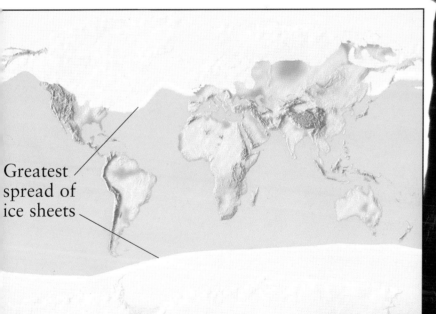

the Great Ice Age, 18,000 years ago, w half of Earth frozen. Mammoths olved woolly coats to cope (right).

ROCKS AND FOSSILS

Information about past climates comes from rocks formed at the time, and fossils – remains of long-dead plants and animals, preserved in rocks and turned to stone. Climate changes were very gradual. Plants and animals could slowly adapt, or spread to more suitable areas. Now, our actions bring fast climate changes.

11

Some people talk about the 'greenhouse effect' as if it's a threat, which it is, but also as though it is new – which it isn't. So what is the greenhouse effect and why is it such a danger to our future?

THE REAL GREENHOUSE EFFECT

Glass lets through light well, but not heat. A garden greenhouse lets in the Sun's light rays. Inside, some of this light energy is reflected or soaked up by objects, and naturally converted to heat or infra-red rays. This warmth is then trapped inside the glass and builds up, making the greenhouse hotter from within.

Hot topic
Earth with its natural greenhouse effect is 30°C warmer than without it. But that's a tiny amount compared to planet Venus. Most of the atmosphere there is carbon dioxide, which is a very effective greenhouse gas. It's so efficient at trapping heat that the average temperature on Venus is an incredible 470°C – hot enough for wood to catch fire. Studying Venus can help scientists to predict what could happen here.

'Hot-house' Venus.

The average temperature over the whole Earth through an entire year is 15°C. Without the natural greenhouse effect to trap the Sun's energy, it would be minus 15°C!

THE NATURAL GREENHOUSE EFFECT

Earth's atmosphere is a mixture of gases, mainly nitrogen (78%) and oxygen (21%), plus tiny amounts of argon, carbon dioxide and others. Some of the Sun's energy which is not heat, is absorbed and converted into heat, in the atmosphere and at the surface. This raises the overall temperature, but only to a certain level. Above this level, more heat would be lost into space than is received from the Sun, so Earth would cool again. In the natural greenhouse effect, energy in balances energy out.

On a sunny day inside a real greenhouse or glasshouse, it may be 20°C warmer than outside. This is not due to the Sun's heat coming in, but to its light, which is changed to heat.

Reflected by clouds back into space.
20%

Incoming heat, light and other energy from the Sun (solar radiation)
100%

Reflected by gases in atmosphere back into space.
6%

Absorbed by clouds and gases in the atmosphere.
19%

Absorbed by land and water at Earth's surface.
51%

Reflected by Earth's surface directly back into space.
4%

EARTH'S GREENHOUSE EFFECT

Earth is like a greenhouse, but with gas rather than glass. Some of the Sun's non-heat energy is changed into heat, and trapped by greenhouse gases in the atmosphere. This has occurred in a steady, balanced way for a very long time. But ... (see next page).

13

Earth's natural greenhouse effect is becoming unnatural. We pump huge amounts of heat-trapping gases into the air. It's like wrapping Earth in a thick blanket. Disastrous results include global warming (see following pages).

THE MAIN BLAME

Carbon dioxide, CO_2, makes up only 0.03% (1/3,000th) of the atmosphere. But it is an effective greenhouse gas, it traps a lot of heat. Every form of burning produces CO_2 and this is the main reason its levels are rising rapidly.

WHICH GASES WARM MOST?

Carbon dioxide is important because we produce so much of it daily. But chlorofluorocarbons, CFCs, trap 20,000 times more heat than carbon dioxide. They are used in refrigeration and air-conditioning equipment, industrial cleaners and to make foam-type packaging.

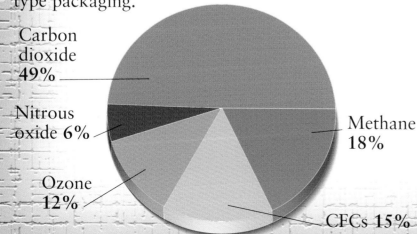

Carbon dioxide 49%

Nitrous oxide 6%

Ozone 12%

Methane 18%

CFCs 15%

General industry 24%

In an industrialized nation such as the USA, over one-third of the CO_2 released into the atmosphere is from burning fuels like gas, coal and oil to generate electricity. Almost as much comes from petrol, diesel, jet and other engines, in various forms of transport. Factory furnaces and ovens account for about one-quarter. Home central-heating, stoves and fires add around one-tenth.

Transport 30%

Hot topic

Clearing forests is a double disaster for the climate. Burning the unwanted wood creates one-fifth of global CO_2. Living trees take in CO_2 and use it for growth – but not when they are gone.

Forest trees help to lower CO_2 in the atmosphere.

Power stations 35%

Homes 11%

MORE PROBLEM GASES

Other heat-trapping gases include nitrous oxide, especially from coal-fired power stations, and ozone, produced in smog over traffic-choked cities. Another is methane. It comes from burnt wood, and is made naturally by decay, in bogs and swamps, and by digestion in plant-eating animals.

Cows, sheep and other plant-eaters puff methane from their rear ends. More farm animals = more methane.

15

Since we began measuring temperatures accurately, the warmest year in the world was 1998, followed by 2001. It is likely that these records will be broken.

MOUNTING EVIDENCE

Increasing amounts of greenhouse gases in the atmosphere (see previous page) are making our world hotter. This is called global warming. Some people still insist that it has not begun and may never start. But it's here, now. Average world temperatures have risen by over half a degree Celsius in the past 100 years.

Hot topic

More than half of the world's biggest cities are next to the sea. Rising waters caused by global warming, combined with tidal surges and bigger waves from stronger storms, could cause catastrophic floods despite sea defences, like London's Thames River Barrier.

WORLD TEMPERATURE

This chart shows the world's average surface temperature each year for the past 150 years. There are small rises and falls here and there, but the general trend is upwards – and up faster.

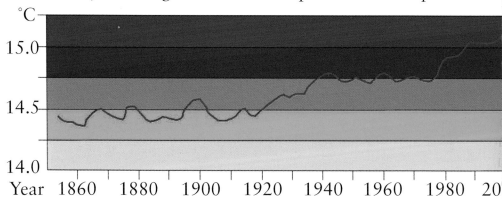

More droughts have affected more regions in the past 30 years, than in the 50 years before. Africa has been hit especially hard. People are already on the edge of starvation, then failed rains bring famines that kill millions. Unlike Africa, developed countries can afford extra water for crops and can buy extra food.

hames Barrier, London.

HOTTER, FASTER

Scientists predict that if we continue making yet more greenhouse gases, global warming will happen faster, by 3 to 5°C in the next 50 years. Even if we stop these gases now, the rise could be 1°C over 20 years. This may not sound much. But it could have devastating effects, for example, by shifting rainfall patterns. What is now rich, well-watered farmland might become parched desert, unable to grow our food.

ICE TO WATER TO FLOOD TO DISASTER

igantic amounts of water re frozen into ice sheets at e poles, especially at ntarctica. As the global arming continues, and ice elts into the ocean, sea vels will rise. Vast areas f land around the world's asts, including great cities d ports, and the homes of illions, are just a metre or o above average sea level. predicted sea-level rise of lf a metre in the next 50 ars will flood so much a-edge land, that half a llion people could be made meless and jobless.

Demonstrators (above) warn of rising seas, and long-term predictions suggest great cities like Miami will drown.

Almost every week there is news of a natural disaster due to violent or unusual weather. Are these events becoming more common?

MORE OFTEN IN MORE PLACES

There have always been gales, tornadoes, hurricanes, downpours and similar powerful weather. But they have increased greatly in recent years. Places where they usually happen are used to coping with some regular damage. But now the events are more destructive, and happen in more places which are unprepared.

In 1988, Hurricane Mitch hit Honduras in Central America and caused huge damage with over 500 deaths.

Many tropical places have regular storms with thunder, lightning and heavy rain. But changes are happening fast as rainfall becomes heavier and winds blow more strongly.

EL NIÑO – 'THE CHILD'

People fishing along South America's west coast noticed that every few years, their catches were much reduced. This is due to changes in a huge ocean current called *El Niño*, 'The Child', because it begins during the Christmas season. Winds and currents combine to bring warmer, nutrient-poor water across the Pacific at the Equator and south to replace the normal cooler, nutrient-rich current that encourages fish.

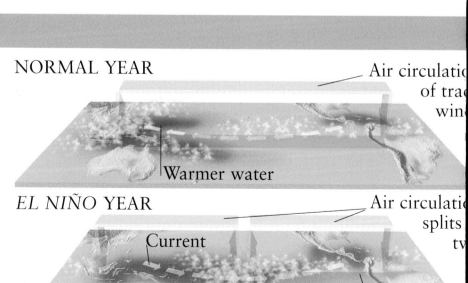

NORMAL YEAR

Air circulatio of tra win

Warmer water

EL NIÑO YEAR

Air circulatio splits t

Current

Warmer water spreads east.

NATURE IN TROUBLE

Global warming is affecting nature too. Flowers bloom earlier in spring, birds migrate later in autumn, and insects that used to sleep through the cold season still buzz about in midwinter. This will also affect people greatly. Mosquitoes, ticks and other warmth-loving pests that carry diseases are spreading into new areas.

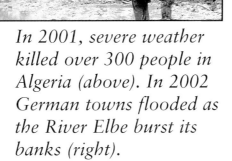

In 2001, severe weather killed over 300 people in Algeria (above). In 2002 German towns flooded as the River Elbe burst its banks (right).

WORLDWIDE EFFECTS OF *EL NIÑO*

El Niño is part of a huge weather system that has effects across the tropics. Droughts affect India (1), Sri Lanka and Indonesia (2), killing crops, and Australia (3), causing bush fires. Cyclone storms hit Pacific islands such as Tahiti (4). Unusually warm water harms coral reefs (5). Downpours and floods affect North America's west coast (6) and the Gulf of Mexico (7), and also South America (8) where the fishing industry is ruined (9). Droughts and floods even hit parts of Africa (10).

Wetter

Drier

Hotter

Equator

1 2 3 4 5 6 7 8 9 10

19

On a clear day, views can be spectacular. But we have fewer clear days now, due to smoke and fumes from power stations, factory chimneys, vehicles and smouldering ex-forests.

Hot topic
Some years ago people campaigned to rid vehicle fuel of lead, since its fumes could cause brain damage. Now attention has shifted to other chemicals and tiny bits called particulates, which damage the lungs.

PARTICULATE POLLUTION

Some of the gases that pollute the atmosphere, such as CFCs (shown on the next page), are invisible. Others, especially exhaust fumes from vehicle engines, carry tiny particulates. These cause a dusty haze, and also chemicals in the fumes react to form smogs that cover cities.

Asian Brown Haze, Bangkok, Thailand.

Cities such as Los Angeles an Mexico City (below) are surrounded by hills. Local cali weather traps vehicle fumes, which change i sunlight into damaging low-level ozone and choking smog.

HARM TO HEALTH

Over the past few years a vast new problem has affected much of India and South East Asia. Called the Asian Brown Haze (see opposite), it is due to weak winds mixing fumes from traffic, power stations, factories, and burning logged forests to clear them for farmland. Millions of people suffer from more asthma, breathing problems and lung infections like bronchitis.

Traffic pollution can kill.

In 1991, the Philippines' Mount Pinatubo volcano erupted, showering the area with thick ash. The ash also blasted high into the atmosphere, to spread around the world and cause two years of cooler, gloomier weather.

21

Ozone is a form of the gas oxygen. Normal oxygen, O_2, makes up one-fifth of air and we must breathe it to stay alive. Ozone, O_3, can be both helpful and harmful, to our climate and our bodies – depending on where it is.

LESS OZONE

The 'ozone layer' is in the atmosphere between 20 and 25 kilometres high. It is not pure ozone but it does contain more ozone than the other layers of atmosphere, mixed in with the normal gases of air. As shown on page 24, the ozone layer protects Earth's surface from the Sun's harmful UV rays, but it is being reduced by gases like CFCs, threatening all living things.

Being GREEN
Sources of CFC gases include aerosol spray cans. The CFCs were used as propellants to force out the contents as a fine spray. Most aerosols now use other propellants and label their cans 'CFC-free' or 'ozone-friendly'. CFCs are also found in fluids in fridge cooling systems. These are also being phased out, but old fridges need careful disposal of CFCs.

A fridges 'mountain' waits for safe disposal of CFCs.

Approved CFC removal.

THE OZONE LAYER AND CFCs

The gases called CFCs 'eat' ozone. Each CFC (1) breaks down in the atmosphere to release its chlorine atom (2). This joins to a molecule of ozone, O_3, (3) and 'snaps off' one of the oxygen atoms to leave normal oxygen, O_2 (4). Then the chlorine releases its oxygen atom, O (5). The single atoms collect and join in pairs to form more normal oxygen (6), while the chlorine is ready to carry out the whole process again (7). The worst-affected area is over the South Pole (left). It is not an empty ozone 'hole' but a depletion or thinning of ozone in its layer.

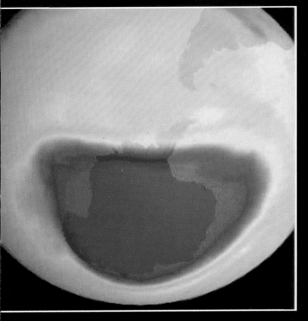

Ozone-poor layer (red) over Antarctica.

Continual loss and production of ozone normally keeps its level steady. Energy in the Sun's rays (A) splits particles or molecules of ozone (B) into normal oxygen molecules (C) and single atoms (D). But these join together to form ozone again (E).

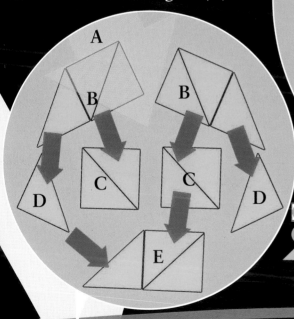

- ▣ CFC
- ◖ Chlorine
- ◥ Ozone (O_3)
- ▨ Oxygen (O_2)
- ▸ Oxygen atom (O)

Ultra-violet rays from Sun

Ozone layer

CFCs from Earth

The Sun sends out, or radiates, many kinds of waves and rays. They include light which plants use to grow, and heat to warm our world. Some of the rays, called ultra-violet (UV), could harm living things. But the ozone layer shields Earth's surface from them.

In space, a suit protects against UV and other rays from the Sun.

THE SUN'S RADIATION

The full range of rays and waves from the Sun is known as the electromagnetic spectrum (right). Most living things on Earth are adapted to cope with these types and amounts of waves. But in less natural conditions, they can be harmful. For example, if light-skinned people are exposed to too much sunshine on tropical holidays, the ultra-violet rays cause painful sunburn.

Gamma rays

X-rays

Ultra-violet

Light

Infra-red (heat)

Micro-waves

Radio waves

Sunburn and too much sunbathing make skin more at risk of conditions such as cancers.

Hot topic

Too much ultra-violet radiation harms not only people, but plants and animals too. At present, the main ozone loss is above the poles, where few people live, and the thinning varies from year to year. But if the loss spreads it could affect millions of people in both northern and southern lands.

Protest against CFC-makers.

LESS MEANS MORE

Less ozone means that more ultra-violet rays are reaching Earth's surface. It is estimated that CFCs, methyl-chloroform and other ozone-damaging gases already in the atmosphere could affect the ozone layer for another 50 years.

OTHER OZONE PROBLEMS

High in the atmosphere, ozone is helpful. But down near the ground it is harmful. In calm, sunny weather, chemicals in traffic fumes undergo changes in sunlight to form ozone-rich smog. Low-level ozone is also a major greenhouse gas (page 14).

Plants damaged by excessive UV include farm crops.

The climate crisis is a worldwide problem. Storms and floods do not stop at a nation's borders. Although all nations suffer, some cause more harm than others.

CARBON IS THE KEY

One way of assessing the problem is by carbon emissions – amounts of carbon dioxide and other greenhouse gases produced by burning. Some places are introducing 'carbon taxes'. If you burn more, you pay more.

Demonstrators dress as famous 'Americans' to protest at the USA's massive contribution to global warming, and its refusal to cut back.

WHO ADDS MOST CARBON?

The USA is by far the biggest air polluter in terms of CO_2. Its high standard of living relies on burning oil-based fuels in power stations, cars, factories and for heating. Each US citizen is, in effect, adding over 20 times more carbon to the atmosphere, than an Indian citizen.

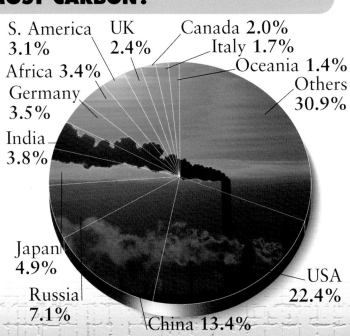

S. America 3.1%
UK 2.4%
Canada 2.0%
Italy 1.7%
Africa 3.4%
Oceania 1.4%
Germany 3.5%
Others 30.9%
India 3.8%
Japan 4.9%
USA 22.4%
Russia 7.1%
China 13.4%

Being GREEN

Satellites 'spy' on the whole globe. They can detect a forest being cleared by burning, which destroys wildlife, and also produces smoke and greenhouse gases. The culprits can be pinpointed and encouraged to become 'greener' in the future.

Satellites: 'spies in space'.

Conservationists use many tactics to publicise problems like global warming. This power station cooling tower in Germany has become a 'screen' for a huge light show.

AN UNFAIR WORLD

Developed countries use up valuable energy sources like coal and petroleum, at a rate that cannot go on forever, when these could be shared among all. Also, as they do so, they pollute the atmosphere for all. International meetings are held to plan schemes where countries emitting most carbon try to reduce it most. But agreements are often weak and do little to solve the crisis.

In 1998, in Kyoto, Japan, the United Nations Climate Conference tried to limit greenhouse gases, but the USA reversed its agreement.

The world is so huge, and its weather is so vast and complicated – can individual people help to clean up the air and restore the climate's natural balance?

ACTIONS AND WORDS

Yes! Many people are not aware of how the crisis will affect their world and their future. Start by spreading information about climate change. Even if we stop releasing all greenhouse and ozone-damaging gases today, world weather will still get hotter and more violent for many years. There's no time to lose.

Hot topic

All types of burning, even renewable 'green' fuels like bio-diesel, make greenhouse gases. Nuclear power is almost zero-emission in this respect. But it has many other problems and possible hazards.

Nuclear is 'non-carbon'.

Volunteers check air purity in the tiny nation of Bhutan, high in the Himalayas. Even on the 'roof of the world' there are pollution problems.

Forests destroyed by logging and clearing are being replanted for the future in the Rishi Valley, in the Chittoor District, in India.

Scientists can genetically modify plants to help them survive in different climates, providing a greener future.

lectric cars cause no air ollution – on the road, t least. But electricity to echarge their batteries generated at power tations, and most of ese pollute the air as ey burn fossil fuels ke coal, gas and oil.

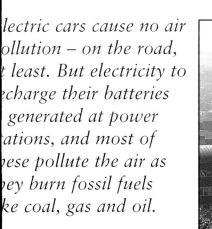

CARBON OUT, CARBON IN

If more carbon-based gases like CO_2 in the atmosphere cause global warming, would less carbon do the reverse? Trees and other plants take in CO_2 from air and energy from sunlight, to live and grow. So forests are 'carbon sinks', moving carbon from the atmosphere to within themselves. It's another good reason to save the trees we have, and plant many more.

29

The climate crisis is very complex. Smog, particle haze, less ozone and more UV rays, excess greenhouse gases leading to global warming, rising sea levels, more violent storms, shifting weather patterns, droughts here, floods there ...

A TRICKY FORECAST

It is impossible to predict how climate change will affect us in the future. Governments need to take action now and maybe our future tomorrows will be brighter and clearer. You can raise awareness of the problems by discussing them in school.

Addresses and websites for further information

WWF
Panda House,
Weyside Park,
Godalming,
Surrey,
GU7 1XR
Tel 01483 426444
www.worldwildlife.org/ climate/
www.panda.org
WWF (formerly WorldWide Fund For Nature) leads efforts to conserve nature and protect the diversity of life on Earth, including addressing the global warming problem.

TIKI THE PENGUIN
www.oneworld.net/ penguin/global_warming/ climate_home.html
Shows younger people how and why the world's getting hotter, what we can do about it, and how it will affect us.

AIR QUALITY (UK)
Freephone Air Pollution Information Service
Tel 0800 556677
www.airquality.co.uk
Information about air quality and pollution in the UK.

AUSTRALIAN GREENHOUSE OFFICE
GPO Box 621,
Canberra ACT 2601,
Australia
Tel 1800 130 606
Fax 02 9274 1390
www.greenhouse.gov.au

EPA GLOBAL WARMING KIDS' SITE
http://www.epa.gov/ globalwarming/kids/
US Environmental Protection Agency's website for younger people, full of information.

FRIENDS OF THE EARTH
26–28 Underwood Street,
London,
N1 7JQ
Tel 020 7490 1555
Fax 020 7490 0881
www.foe.co.uk
The largest international network of environmental groups in the world, campaigning for a greener future, including action to reduce climate change.

UK RIVERS NETWORK
http://www.ukrivers.net/ climate.html
Books, articles and web links about climate change.

GREENPEACE UK
Canonbury Villas,
London,
N1 2PN
Tel 020 7865 8100
Fax 020 7865 8200
E-mail
info@uk.greenpeace.org
www.greenpeace.org.uk
Powerful campaigning organization. Support taking action against those who needlessly contribute to air pollution and climate change.

GLOSSARY

atmosphere
The layer of air that surrounds the planet Earth. It becomes thinner with height, and above 500 kilometres fades away into the vast unknown of space.

CFCs
Chlorofluorocarbons, industrial chemicals which have an especially damaging effect on ozone in the Earth's atmosphere.

climate
Long-term patterns of wind, rainfall, temperature and other aspects of day-to-day weather, that change gradually over many years and centuries.

drought
A long period when little or no rain or other forms of water reach the ground.

environment
The surroundings including soil, rocks, water, air, plants, animals and even man-made structures.

genetic modification
Altering a living thing's genes, which are the basic instructions, in the form of the chemical DNA, for how it grows and survives.

greenhouse gases
Gases that help to trap heat in the atmosphere, causing the temperature of the Earth to rise.

ozone
A form of the gas oxygen, which is spread through the atmosphere and helps to protect Earth's surface against some of the Sun's damaging ultraviolet rays.

radiation
Energy that comes from a source, like the Sun, and travels in waves like UV rays.

smog
A combination of fumes, particles and gases, especially from vehicle exhausts, that causes a harmful haze in the air.